Deilmsttuu
Sedutitlum

Multitudes

Deilmsttuu
Sedutitlum

Margaret
Christakos

COACH HOUSE BOOKS

TORONTO

  Canadá

Published with the generous assistance of the Canada Council for the Arts and the Ontario Arts Council. Coach House Books also gratefully acknowledges the support of the Government of Canada through the Canada Book Fund and the Government of Ontario through the Ontario Book Publishing Tax Credit.

LIBRARY AND ARCHIVES CANADA CATALOGUING IN PUBLICATION

Christakos, Margaret
    Multitudes / by Margaret Christakos. – First edition.

Poems.
Issued in print and electronic formats.
ISBN 978 1 55245 279 0 (pbk.). – 978 1 77056 361 2 (epub)

I. Title.

PS8555.H675M84 2013   C811'.54   C2013-904094-3

Multitudes is available as an ebook: ISBN 978 1 77056 361 2.

Purchase of the print version of this book entitles you to a free digital copy. To claim your ebook, please email sales@chbooks.com with proof of purchase or visit chbooks.com/digital. (Coach House Books reserves the right to terminate the free digital download offer at any time.)

alphabets exist
Inger Christensen, trans. Susanna Nied

Threshold

sing th body electric
Walt Whitman

push words into body.

do those words form a column or spiral?

do those words coalesce as body

into the body they conjure?

push words into mouth.

do those words form a tongue or jetty?

is a probe formed that touches

the tongue it entangles?

push words onto mound of nipple,

onto mounded nipple jewels.

do words circulate as honey, as

tentacles that leaven and stiffen?

are words the door-slab we cross

or the instepping over?

do words think what they want

or rush in, impartial?

fasten words into armpits,

kneebacks, elbow fronts.

do these words moving into view

bulk or break like touch or

are they just its cushions?

do I cock my head sideways

peer along tubal promontories and

at this occult angle drench

my throat in letters?

do I tongue-roll speech?

do I usher words

into corridors we recognize

or do new phrases

fissure the organism?

pack syllables into glands.

deliver glandular phonemes glad to open.

proposition palms moistening

in response.

wave words toward portals

as if bright green pennants.

signal presence at the threshold.

do words gush good manners?

do words think about waiting?

can words hold back or off or away

until the body goes rigid and dirigible?

a warm headwind pushes against the body

the way words do.

words form a column or spiral

of headwind, and it is honeyed.

it is tentacled. it is probing.

words suckle the column and

nipple the mound, delve inside ducts

and shovel out insides.

let's push words into coming.

gnash words into coming, into body.

shove grammar onto parts.

load coming into each.

is it the threshold of coming or

the deep thrash of asking?

I wonder do words have any clue.

I wonder if words hold me

or if you do.

maybe there's zero here

save our so-green thresholds.

Hoop

Bitch, bitch, bitch.
Maude, *Maude*

meaning,

moaning

moaning,

meaning

[rpt.]

LOVE SONG

in u

i nu

nous

no us

SUBSTITUTION SONG

no we

now e

sehcrul

    dnarts

        detavele

          htiw

            tarantula

               seilleb evisolpxe

   kcolf

       detanod

         gniyap

           oiranecs

              stib

                 sselriah

  erutaN sa elbavol

      dehctitsni

     tnuocca

        yuqolilos

            tn'ac

              sugahpose fo

                 [etc.]

BRINGING

In bringing in this gorilla

which lurches in2 soliloquy

This gorilla's bewildered

This gorilla has a body so different ...

it can't b in th room

lacking or having

a strand of esophagus

garnished in something timid

This elephant

This shark, mastodon

Purple loosestrife n leeches

elevated in an elevator

then vapour.

It's a room, in

camera with polyester,

fluorescence, aluminum

Park squirrels bioswarm th fibreglass

everybody knows it's inebriating

There's alutnarat

U wake one morning Phyllis

Diller wrestles a lion, familial reunion, then

voluminous fire gulfs or engorges

th community centre Local bricks

with explosive bellies arrow

Toxic smoke talks abt how lovable we r it

won't shut up but exudes ...

different

deeffinrt

tnereffid

Rows of chairs engrommetted in a factory

backroom so workers can surf

People online n chew Nicorettes It's

adolescent lemur stuck in th stall

sideways Flock of

cormorants n juice boxes

donated by Nestlé Sleeves bleached

properly Antihistamines distributed

impressive Seniors paying federal

taxes without question.

I so enjoy breathing alongside

a scenario of refuge when 2 zoo-born

giraffes go up in a figure 8

firework, limegreen leaf bits

showering a petite rainfall on

my April hairless forearm.

We r as abellov as Nature is.

There r flecks of sanguinity in our sideburned

quietude, dusky institched voices while mature elk herds

ligature the building lobbing homeopathy against

multiple extinction rumours This Dictaphone

this Morse

this Spirograph Kaypro n Letraset

peel black its backing

then poster Burn ur bra

Take back th night Hold others 2 sluggish

account Believe in rainforest

4 th trees 4 what they r

bringing in –

In bringing in this gorilla

which lurches in2 soliloquy

This gorilla's bewildered

This gorilla has a body so different

it can't b in th room

lacking or having

a strand of esophagus

garnished in something timid

If it could b, it would arise that way, but I think we agree

it cannot.

Haey, u know

who is watching, hippie-girl. I fit in2

u like a waist

inside a hoop yahe yaeh hyae

Famous waist, a

hula hoop, she loves u

ahye haye yeah.

If melancholia, or pleasure, encircles, with its rhythmhtyhr

n its ringingnignir

as long as it is gnivomoving, it

displaces a plain 1970s telling.

But I don't think melancholia, or

pleasure, is th problem exactly. I'm thinking

ur summoning a park

around that hoop, n a city

around that park, n concentric rings of wifi around that city

n well y wouldn't u with those magique

contempo-hips

which r a nuisance

th multitudes want 2 ride under, actually, I'm not dead yet, sister,

or have u riding us.

After all, bodies beckon bodies with their gninaomoaning.

I wonder if th immediate seesaw ng of th present

in a half-kempt hipster park

is th hula hyae ehay heay

is th hoop that

rather than encircling u

keeps ur cunt far from th commons, 4

we know it's not just me on my rickety bench, a *poet* 4 god's sake,

performing something really special n

                    retro.

THE FOLLOWING USER
[SAYS THANK YOU TO MN RENOVATOR FOR THIS USEFUL POST:]

Warm air: A = in, B = in. Hot water: A = out,
B = in. Electric: A = in, B = out. Turns on th blower

as soon as flames 4 heat. From a drafty back study
central exposed front room well away from th windows.

I was having exactly th same old n malfunctioning
problem. Ur own personal load-test data is maybe switching

some pre-set limit. Don't forget is something
we should do right LOL. So there I go re-engineering a gizmo

that isn't broken again with short plenum 8 cm below
th damped-off joints. Colder air is denser more oxygen

n slits fresh. Inducer has vibration 2 it but I cranked
2 Hi. I just KNOW somebody's going 2 tell me 2 check

th manual.

IT'S LIKE I COULD DO SOMETHING

for Lena Dunham

it's like i could do something with my voice i couldn't do b4 because it's
not clear 2 me y i should feel any differently n bsides i paid 4 this with my
own money i earned it ergo it's mine / there's some consistency u just
want 2 watch out 4 if u r th bad friend so much harder than comfortable n
dripping abt th waistline since anyone over 18 has th option of a
buy-back plan / put those words out there n i'm not responsible 4 their
blank lotto tickets n vandalized subway stations / simple statements like a
hangover jog up an offseason boardwalk or like th stench of lilies around
easter *yecchh* chisel my patience / th point was impropriety – urs – being
kissed at dusk n loving it so th junkie downstairs cd hear everything that
was messy n inarticulate regarding major plans 4 th webcam / th other
thing u need 2 know right abt now is that i might b extricating myself from
this collapsing resto deal as a person has 2 stay in th clear n narrow of
their own generational aspirations / a person has only those near around
him 2 care 4 when it comes right down 2 that last commuter train 2 th end
of th line that crosses over its own shortcut

i hope i'm not unmaking myself invisible!

i hope i'm erasing what u liked abt me because it's suffocating 2 b tender n
in ur fat spot with e-readers you've propagated across th sunrise in a
whole other time zone *in a whole other time zone* when rates r lowest n
several custodians here r eating canned macaroni that's seriously putrid /
there's abt 15 minor phonetical conjunctions i might lift n resuscitate in an
entirely gutted soho gallery space but have 2 say there's a lot on my mind
that u can't necessarily hear me thinking – u just have 2 trust me on that
one like u just have 2 trust my sense of timing n my pretty excellent

boundaries

That poet

That poet was not

That poet was not an emperor

That poet was not an emperor wearing

That poet

That poet was wearing something

That poet was not an emperor wearing nothing

That poet was trying 2 get something

That poet had a line n some hoopla

Had th voice of a generalist n dungarees on his knees

That poet had a beat

A streetbeat

That poet had eyes like beads

Like little black beads

That poet was wearing a few sequins

That poet was clothed in

That poet was a frequent poet

That poet used 2 b John Barlow

That poet used 2 stop himself in th middle of a long line n giggle

That poet knew what was a longing line n what was a place to stop it

He could quench it

That poet was not an emperor

That poet was plum naked

That poet knew nothing useful n everything else

That poet had his clothes on all right

That poet was tightrope-teetering on2 his next languorous lingo

That poet was crossing all sorts of giddy ponderings

When's th last time u heard him

That poet

That poet was no emperor

That poet John Barlow.

I remember back in th day

I remember back in th Walt vault

Who do we have 2 subpeona 2 get John Barlow back onstage

Who do we need on our panel

What poet knows th poet who knows John Barlow

What poet

What's th point of that poet

What do u get out of th way when u get that poet

What do u want 2 get from me here, right now

What song

What old saw

What cool hula trickery with th alphabet

Tell me what u want

Tell me when u want it, people

I am not an emperor

I am wearing my dungarees

I am ready to workshop

I am here so plum

So naked n jiggling

CITY HALL (TORONTO) 2012

for Jack Layton

1

Almost

nobody wants it

t/here now. Expanse or courtyard, field encased

concrete, flattened plain perfect 4 crowd control.

Array th horses eh.

Riot lines enter westward. Lasers' aim, crosscutting vulnerable

capital. Th Moore. Th arcs. Hoses could pump foam, fell

leather uppers. Martial snipers let's face it would

have an absolute field day.   Encircle

n stride.   Traverse.

Everybody gets de-authoritative. Entire ethnicities used 2 bbq

like there's no tomorrow.

One by one business people cross th eradicated

square. Nobody wants. No mirrors anywhere. Or chalk.

Civic property that belongs 2

no one. Why protest what's empty?

2

Array horses 4 everyone.

Riot lines can bbq.

Split t/here.

Civic property that belongs 2 no one.

When do u. Wants nobody.

Why protest. Mirrors anywhere.

3

encircle n stride. traverse. stride n traverse, encircle.

why protest what's empty. what belongs 2 no one.

traverse stride n encircle. stride encircle traverse.

everybody wants authoritative. recall civic. Jack memory.

encircle. traverse n stride. absolute field day.

riot lines enter westward or courtyard, field encased.

almost anybody t/here. expanse of a threshold. when do we.

Stride

Encircle

Converse.

4

There's no   mirrors   anywhere.   No

empty **WHAT?**

Tomorrow   just   one

repurposed **WHAT DO?**

Square of thresholds.

With citizenly   footsteps.   Split.   Recall **WHAT DO WE?**

Jack.   Civic   memory.   Everybody   gets

entire.   Our **DO WE WANT?**

Citizenly   field day.   Enter

westward,   **WHAT DO WE?** crosscutting

WANT? expanse   or **WHEN DO WE?**

courtyard **WANT IT?**

NOW.

Perfect   4   CROWD

NOW.

Perfect   4   CROWD

NOW.

Perfect   4   CROWD

CIRQUIT

something abt rings of people

forming round a residential neighbourhood

ready to lob fiery blobs

n burn all th houses

flat; gathering my beloveds in2

a van awheel in circles

thru streets, adding another beloved,

another, another, 5 hrs passing

n still not on th

hiway outta here.

Enough

y wd i nd   wd i nd 2   i nd 2 spk   nd 2 spk 2

2 spk 2 u?   spk 2 u? y   2 u? y wd   u? y wd i

Even breezes gather assiduous from rear alley.

But wait several moments.

I want memory specific and positive.

A few syllables mince secure yet clean outcome.

Watch: A poetics of observation wins awards.

Turn gather fester rally wait wait mince secure watch deadline.

Be alone LOL. When online

nominate yourself.

Here's the lament [status update] of the afternoon:

Across arteries clogged with traffic I

sought a coffee with the public, you know. Coffee!

Overheard strains of iTunes leaking

past headphones hatting streetcar riders

[client customer consumer user].

Someone's knapsack dumped onions, blocked EXIT.

Market index indicated major losses.

A kid reported an earache. *Quoi?* Half the carload

swatted dust from screens.

No one spoke. The light was blue.

No one spoke. Blue light.

No one spoke. Or:

A teenager spoke on her cellphone about fucking a fucking moron
    douchebag last night and now she was going to Sephora.

No one listened.

Everyone belonged.

Why would I need to speak to you?

Show your transfer. Call

the code on the pole.

                              Everything blue

                              everything light

                              everything you

                                 want at

                                hand there

                                  is no

1

While I was waiting you may think I have forgotten you.

In this case we hurriedly move to efface the pronouns.

After the past festers imagining built on purity.

Everyone slips.

There's crust.

Fortunately cities are large striped with busy.

Few speak of crosslights.

Or are these critics?

Recently I heard about writers who intend to disappear in their texts.

Some want to mount a novel civilization.

Both feel regal.

Is memory assiduous?

Is an image named you the clamp in whose tough metal I insist my own gloss?

For example, I see you at the market with one arm raised to manage the
    weight of a bag of onions.

The seller nods and with a slight push passes.

Very economical.

See how closely I spy how promptly I reappear.

Does a beloved matter?

You load your onions into a dark cloth knapsack and now you are carrying
significant organic weight on your completely darling spine.

I was such a shit I mince and observe from the rear.

At the intersection strangers produce near-erasable gestures of notice.

One's iris squeezes around the post of an earring.

One's lower lip demi-lowers.

One's suck.

One's freeze.

Then forget it everybody jerks and walks their earbud cords bob spritely.

Possibly affection crusts over.

I pay with my bank card at the confectionery no one resorts to speaking.

There's a statement in the mail.

Such good bedtime stories.

Transactions recoverable for ease of.

But somebody must snooze.

Imagining's slips.

So the thing is while I sleep even my head is silent, so we have no record
of how I may dream of you, my revenant.

Onions are anguish, common coding.

Me piling such on your spine ever wishful.

Off balance.

You just slice them up to cook.

Few speak of crosslights.

Sometimes it is kind.

Crusts of bread slush up the curb.

I have ardent cramps.

This can be ridiculed by anyone who doesn't.

Will you participate? In ridicule?

Have you asked this of your own torso?

So one day the weight of very nice onions slowed you in the bike lane.

Somehow a kid stumbled.

This was in a video game.

Near collision.

You braked to avoid a we on the black pavement.

Suddenly *ohs*, eyes ricochet crazy.

There are writers who record the overprotection of the G20.

One gorges.

Others gouge.

Some really like metaphors for their main course.

We hurry to lift the boy back into his sneakers.

Imagine the strange violence of the virtual moment these shoes dislodge.

Can you resume your bike route?

I hurry with my panier half-open.

Of course if even a little it is open.

So how I hurry involves an open panier and a wind entering.

In this way me.

Adequate force is even breezes.

I feel this no one else has to feel this ever or in the video game for me to
feel this on my face.

3

Cubed then translucent.

It's luck.

Slips to particles.

Hidden under a bed and dust pretend in SimCity.

I pretend a lot of stuff about you.

Rotate your earring posterior.

Somebody retaliates with a cross-check across the kneecap.

I push my credit card into a stranger's fly.

Ismem or yassidu.

Yes perhaps it is all right to admire sestinas.

A couple counts vowels.

One's grammar.

Gut real irrelevant in the mailbox for several bucks.

Forget we averaged how I waited, all my waiting for not you but some
images of you I like to pretend are congealing in the bar fridge.

That's the main confession.

Flickering traffic lamps seem to lack.

Its most obvious production.

I get it, we is no enigma of note.

Forgotten.

Torso your.

These are only onions.

This was even compost.

Larding is the event of we.

Still, here's a

                    gathering.

1

There's crust, an image named you. See how closely
a beloved matters, dark cloth knapsack.
This can be ridiculed with my half-open panier. Slips
to particles, so I push my credit card to admire sestinas.
Congealing in the bar fridge imagining built
on purity. A slight push passes
writers who intend to disappear in their texts.
Why would I need near-erasable
violence of the virtual moment? See how
I hurry, how promptly the past festers and how
very economical. Adequate force. Will you
participate for me to feel this on my face?
I feel this and no one else has to feel this
ever or in the high-def video game.

2

In a moment for a moment there is a moment I call inspired

when I tweet about what I feel and want on my cheek

the force of even breezes

that I want to gather for a few syllables. You are

what I have forgotten while I compose the text small

enough, economical and funny, stingingly

savvy or angled to cause undeniable media stir.

If I have forgotten it is only because she bores me

with pompous statuses of complaint and trivial

indigestion. But wait, there's another photo

of the day she got her septum pierced and how

renewed now am I. I am some aperture.

You are the arsenal. Koo koo

kachoo you later. Or are these critics?

Are you a critic?

Recently I read about a victim whose half-bitten nose

because I am privy to up-to-the-minute news updates

take their chunk out of me, they really do, when I remember

you or the clamp in whose tough metal I insist

my own gloss.

3

No enigma of note. A slight push then in my palms

cold onions to place on your eyes burned

from the tear gas cops shot as a warning. You'd better.

Is memory assiduous? See

how closely I spy. Sometimes

it's kind. That's mainly confession.

For example. Off balance. Near collision. One's grammar. Feel regal.

No one resorts to speaking. I was such a shit

I mince and observe from the rear.

Some say a poetics of witness is enough or not quite

enough. Traffic lamps flutter and seem to

forget it everybody jerks and walks their

cords

bob

spritely.

Weapon

No lyric no cry.
January 20, 2012 at 19:48

A Note by

on Monday, September 11, 2010

at 8:59 Cerise, however did

you learn to form your

Qs with such an open

heart??? Wick A Note by

on Monday, September

11, 2008 at 8:57 Possibly,

I did. But you always

take your great-aunt's word with

much too stiff a gum.

Con the group into liking

your shortbread. That's my best

advice on the whole fricassee.

Spiffy A Note by

on Monday, September 11, 2005

at 8:55 All right then,

Christopher-Tom, have your tailor

call my grocer and we'll

hammer out a deal we

can both live with. Fra

Pitooey A Note on Monday,

September 11, 2003 at 8:54

Gertrude, Are you sure you

can't make just one sentence

smell like savory? Please? Your

best hound, Crawbelly. A Note

Monday 8:53 Darling Henry, Do

you think you'll have time

to fix the garage door

in time for Samantha's wedding

rehearsal? It is September after

all! Know you're verrrrry busy,

interesting to view how over the past several years fb

has become a magazine in fact THE magazine where contributors

link each other to 'content'

vast over the web consolidating

interest communities Selves market self

The bits where 'friends' say

something about her day or how he's feeling affirm the

larger comfort of belonging in an emotional network but the

                                                    holy hottt
                                                    babez :')

majority of posts now seem to be acts of alternative

journalism being performed for assumed allies You do this 'for

free' to constitute subjective reality

shifts within a radically more

virtual 'norm' and to vie

against the extinction of my

own vocations They all seem to believe in yourselves as

readership Curious and curiouser it competes for her first stirrings

chubmeister
city del pls

in the morning It is practically the last consumption of

each day It behaves like a social life but gradually

erases a social life as

much as it creates one

'I' in your third person

feels you are speaking to a

'them' but day by day some of us become more

untranslatable about picking up the phone as if the mirror-glass

o gawd bin th
fatroll

will crack perhaps most reticulate in mind this season is

how fb generates a theatre of people-ideas the idea of

x the idea of y

translated head to head almost

without voice As if each

accompanies each other soothingly without

the cordial stickiness of physical companionship He streams near each

other's idea of each other without the sloppy attention-onus of

tit fail dp now

i mean it)))

mutually sustaining embodiment You edit and edit and edit She

edits You decide what you'll edit When he's spontaneous I

edit that in for an

allowable waft When you're sick

with fear you're never sick

with fear They edit so

there is no I and don't want to be, sort of,

alone

Distances brows lip height weight colour shade pallor age where what
    footwear

Key squeal groans versions events report information outcome private
    website pride

Self hands weapon backyard fence uncle glove knee station details
    sequence conscience shut-eye morning coffee front desk

Deeds allegiances enough one visit really fun night

Foramoment, Iturnedtothewindow

Iturnedand

ForamomentwhenIturnedIgatheredinformation

Thewindowwasgone

Therewasaplaceoflightinaplaceoflight

Wasashadedrawn

To detail multitudes we use

the distance between brow and

lip To detail multitudes we

zoom To detail multitudes you

count arrange by height I

weigh To detail multitudes we

think in colour shade pallor

age To detail multitudes I

squint I size up You

recall who was standing where

and in what footwear I

think in the key of

squeals and groans.

I call in my version

of events I try to

be specific and unflinching I

report You offer as much

information as you possibly can

for the good of all

concerned To secure a positive

outcome we think it through

in private and then visit
their website You swallow your
pride and fess up You
feel you should You want
to live with yourself after
all To sort out whose
hands held the weapon you
try pantomime in your backyard.

I push you into the fence and you cry uncle.

I throw the glove at
your knee You lose You
need to get down to
the station in haste Go
now so details stay crisp
persist in sequence Leap Let
your conscience breathe sleep get
some shut-eye First thing in
the morning get dressed Something
comfortable yet clean Skip coffee.

Show up at the front
desk Simply say I want

to help as much as

I can begin to detail

multitudes We do the deed

to redeem Clarify my allegiance

You were mistaken it was

a really fun night Once

is enough suffice will

have to

OBVI

When you're sick with fear you're never sick with, or,

You're sick with fear you're never sick, or,

Sick with fear you're never, or,

With fear you're, or,

Fear is my motherfuckin best 'friend,' jks

Foramoment, you

Turnedtothewinnings

Youturnedand. The

Doughwasgone. For

Amomentwhenyou

Turnedyougatheredinformation

Therewasacoin

Oflightin

Placeoflight

Shadesdrawn

THE FITFUL EVENTS

These come to me days and nights and go from
me again, / But they are not the Me myself. — WW

We drive for half hour come to barns with
cows a merry go round. En route we'd passed
a falls. Boats bobbed. We opted to
stop. You extracted basket from trunk unpacked
picnic. Ants gushed out small hill near
my sandal. I squished many torsos.
Little legs wafting eyelashes ephemeral
loss. Another roadtrip we sought RV lot. You
hoped to trade up. I came along for the french
fries. Inside polyurethane surfaces smelled, everything
glued shut. I suggested sleeping in there might induce
asthma. You looked over my baseball cap nostrils
twitching. For once I thought maybe we didn't make such
a good match, me, your straw. About twenty thousand
fans made a noise mass riot in action. I
couldn't see players' faces yet felt
seats surge. That was some drum kit, triple
drum I think. You'd stuffed toilet paper into ear
cavities drank gin cooler waved at me
from time to time. Thumbs up. Thumbs way up.
Gravel path gradually lost grit soon we rode tar.
About two thirds distance across bridge
hatchback stalled. You started shrieking at guy next to
us, at me. You said I resembled my baby
picture. Were not in control of your slurs. I

threw up next tried to climb out of car okay
taxi happened by. So I solved
all that needed solving that
evening. You got left for once, ha! A pinkish
spring day about 2 p.m. deep nasturtium beds
flamed. Sky flickered blue. Kid waddled near with
balloon dog. Thing about balloon dogs they don't
last. Two adults hovered tad angry. I figured
it was good thing I couldn't get preggers. You
scrape water with paddle simply hack into
river pray wooden hull shoots forward
slingshot. In quiet bar waiter lights our
tea light offers free martinis glass dish
cashews. Several women strip writhe. You pass me
proxy I sign in extra-winding script
tug at my neck until tie relents. Thank god
I whisper. All these people fit their times
all these places held form. All these events
hoisted away from my body a keyboard
I'd again moisten from afar.

2 d tain multitudes Th Connors use th distance

b tween brow ... Philip zooms 2

d tain multitudes Peter n Cathy Werner count by

height n Mr Groening weighs 2 d tain multitudes th

Panachawks think in colour multitudes Van Quentin squints

Larry R sizes up M Penant recalls who

was in what footwear n Ric Hinta thinks

in th key of squeals n Katie S

website so Mrs Constantine swallows her middle daughter

Jessica R's pride fessing up n Thierry N

...

Schumacher's pantomime in his backyard n Pierre G

pushes Joy L into th fence Joy L

cries uncle Pierre G throws Joy L's losses

2 Th Kanes get 2 th station in

haste Go now ... let Miss Ninten's conscience sleep

first morning get clean Coffee front desk n

report crime know ... The Brothers Chang deed

n redeem Mr Allen Abernathy's allegiances since

wazza really fun night Once will have 2

do 4 th persons d tained

Forseveralmoments, weturnedfromthewindows

Therewereshadesdrawn

Weturnedand

Forseveralmomentswhenweturnedwegathered

Inmorphation

Thedoorsweregone

Therewereplacesoflightsinplacesoflights

STATUS

We were all seeking

more in formation on morphology

we wanted faces with names

we wanted names with faces

O to be both recognizable and a bit of an identity dervish.

It is a pleasure

to be informed

to be in good form facing each other

to recognize patterns of shade and light

to gravitate toward the details

the little dimple so unique

the crow's feet

all your wonky teeth

your zany hairline

how you look at your best;

And when you splinter on some retail camera

clutching contraband, we have

to repost.

Interesting 2 view over th past selves market

self. Something about belonging – 2 b specific n

unflinching – performed. 2 vie against ourselves 4 our

first stirrings – 2 sort out whose hands held

th weapon. Babez :') speaking 2 u as if

th mirror-glass – leaps, lets conscience breathe –

accompanies without

th cordial stickiness of each other, that attention-onus –

one was mistaken, 4 it was really quite fun.

Well, we edit an allowable waft sick with

fear – one visit will have 2 do – 2 persist in sequence

elone.

Mounds

No, *u* r th bad friend.
Hannah, *Girls*

Cold side walk

Acdd eikl losw

Acddei kllosw

Wake hard dawn

Aaad dehk nrww

Aaadde hknrww

Aaaa cddd deeh ikkl lnor swww

Aaaacd dddeeh ikklln orswww

Wwwsro nllkki heeddd dcaaaa

Crow call ache / soon step past

Aacc cehl lorw / aeno opps sstt

Aaaccc eehlln oooppr sssttw

Wttsss rppooo nllhee cccaaa

Poor rain morn / wake slow cold

Aimn nooo prrr / acde kllo osww

Aacdei kllmnn ooooop rrrsww

Wwsrrr pooooo nnmllk iedcaa

Part 2

Ww ws ro nl lk ki he ed dd dc aa aa

Wt ts ss rp po oo nl lh ee cc ca aa

Ww sr rr po oo oo nn ml lk ie dc aa

www www tts sss srr rrr

ppp ooo ooo ooo nnn nml

lll llk kki ihh eee eed

ddd dcc ccc aaa aaa aaa

Part 3

aaaa aaaaaccc ccdd ddde

eeee

hhii kkkl lllllmnn nnoo

oooo

ooop pprr rrrs sssttww

wwww

cold sidewalk wake hard

dawn

crow call achesoon step

past

poor rain morn wakeslow

cold

walkwa

esoons

oorrai

akeslo

DOCK

Wavering on a stoop. The day doesn't start yet. Days on end come to a stop. The water is all in the lake. Level rises, falls, but the lake is itself. Everything alive in the lake belongs. Anything incompatible immediately ceases to breathe. There's a limit.

You don't necessarily do what is strategic when moths fly into your lips. What if the mouth had been ajar. What if I'd swallowed that fly. Perhaps I'll dive under the surface.

I was an old lady in the first dream. Then I woke in a hotel room with tartar sauce on my little finger. We'd had supper and fucked. I didn't feel so old then.

Kids are obsessed with opening and shutting any door they find, rushing their shoulders through every portal. What happens that it locks? How will I escape? They spend a decade deciding which way to run when the walls close in. They're smart. Days don't end when they sleep.

Lake streams around the rockpoint the way you penetrated me in gladness. Crappy bedspread didn't matter. We weren't looking at the patterns. Wind reverses direction and heads out to the hillside way over there, by the hospital. That place is full of windows stuck shut. Bad air. You think twice about going in there for the X-ray. Maybe you'll never come out.

Sign a DNR before you leave the nurses' station, we really can't leave this undecided. Pack up all your shit, hit the highway and get yourself free of all you can't abide; or, kick your shins forward and find some nutrition at the lake's bottom. Haul it forth and feed the masses inside you dying by the minute from gentle disappointment. Make a fucking choice, howabout.

Most of the silence you hear here is suffocated yelling. Just saying. I watch the train back up around the bend, swallowing its own metal hum.

People consider it a good move when violence is zeroed out of tolerance. True, things are cleaner, less blood to mop, less breakage. Nobody mentions, though, how tough it is for a body to sift through the void. To get a handle on the vacuum. Suck it up, they suggest. Suck it up.

When I use a category like People I'm probably hiding in the juniper, excessively chewing.

Tradition has it a few locks of hair are left on the tombstone. Subtle. I'd gnawed off a forearm, figured it was best to jog clear of the gravedigger who likes to flirt with all the widowed. He caught up with me, in his mudcaked galoshes, waving my limb like a dog bone. It was embarrassing. All right, here, I conceded, cut off a curl already. Arrange it the way the normal mourners would. Lady, he winks, no can do without tip. By tip, I mean favour, or some solid kindness, you've still got one good arm.

I realized then I was writing an Atwood poem from 1978. Nobody says how brilliant and mean she was, how shitkicking. She'd have known what to say, exactly what to do with that arm.

DISPLAY

th cunt with ankle ties

beige jute string clean

cotton canvas simple

wedge sole

n summer

bareassed on a walkabout

wear ur espadrilles

in th city 4 style

spill ur slender insteps

2 th sun n cocks

arrayed in public

after noon

Pre-digital. Post-analogue. Pre-

9/11. Post-

suicidism.

Pre-pubescent,

post-hysteric.

@ 15 girls.

@ 15 women.

@ 15 breasts surface, suggesting they r in there already, mounds

abt 2 move from behind th ribs

2 on top, like portholes.

@ 15 cunts under th tunic.

Nuts undescended yet sensory.

Tissue masses in motion n all th women @ 15 in 2012

dressing like slavegirls with flat sandals

n exposed toes.

> O I'll b back b4 long. I'm only
>
> 15. What do I
>
> [Bobby Lee, Ode 2 Billy Joe, 1976]

know of th world? [...] But th girl

says no 4 3½ pages! No no no no

No no

No no no no no no

No no no.

Pre-yes. Post –

An arrangement has been made 2 appease th gods. Th in-laws.

Th community leaders. Us.

Hey girl,

it's time 4 u 2 go.

Swim there n shut up. Hide in reeds,
burrow in sand. Doesn't matter how u disappear.
Unlike it.
Or.
Expect th inescapable. Ur
era has prepared u, no?
Bleed on this rock 4 me, come on.
Like it. Like it like
a muthafuckah.
Like it like moonwork.
That's a high-def red that can't b faked, bee-atch.
That's th best red
2 please a god
fast. Please us with ur postings. We
deserve so much more than ur boney ass can ever give us
unupdated. Like it.
Like it with ur red mouth open, red eye
widened. Let th last shutterclick of th world
hit our dickshores, leave us blind.
Or else. Swim 4 it.
4 ur life. 2 that hunk of rock out there. There's no dish.
It's bare earth engulfed in pure seafoam.
Nightmama of nothing of silent
unlike. Ur a strong babywhore
of th 21st century, right?

Choose.

gninaemeaningninaemeaningninaemeaningninaemeaningninae

moaning

If in n sofaras theres

a glass that will hold

well, yo, my guest, ill

bring u water. cold itll

b.

February 23, 2012 at 15:45

Banish

Do women have to be naked
to get into the Met. Museum?
Guerrilla Girls, 1989–

1. BANISHED. ABDEHINS. BA NI SH ED. DE. HS. IN. AB.

B_____d.

anishe.

__nish__.

____ish__.

Ban_hed.

_an_he_.

_a__hed.

_a__sh_d.

____sh__.

____ish__.

Ban_____.

Ba_____d.

____she_.

____he_.

B_____e_.

Go 2 an in-spot

n ask 4 callus

remover. Show ur skin.

Wash ur skin. Take

away some of it

[ur skin], then swab

with rubbing alcohol. Waft

ur scent when u

leave.

Don't overthink it ur probably

not th first one who's

ever felt that. I was

worried abt being tossed out

on my tush. I was

nervous I'd b denuded. When

I went 2 sleep @

night I garnished with my

teeth. Like a crow with

a past. Loosen up! Each

store window discounted. Even though

u tried 2 laugh off

80% of the pain, u

still felt chopped down @

th knees. Initially breadcrumbs were

there, then they weren't. I

scoured th ground that'd bred

me. It was unsprinkled. Tell

some worstgut jokes n get

out of here. There's a

huge crowd in th atrium

c? Large throng by th

turquoise pool, c? I'm a

human whsprr n th humans

don't want me whsprng anymore.

4 I do not call

one greater n one smaller.

I laugh @ what u

call dissolution, n I know

th amplitude of time. I

do not say these things

4 a dollar or 2

fill up th time while

I wait 4 a boat.

A crow all ruffled by

the rain just parked on

a ledge I happen 2

b sitting on th other

side of my window from.

I'd rather say this on

Twitter because then u might

hear me. Is anybody out

there? Like Waters I was

a teenager once. Was one

of th viled. Buildings arrayed

around courtyard. Outside th compound

r ordinary folks going 2

work. Who friggin gives a

shit if. They ask u

politely 2 leave th hospital

as u no longer have

anything they can cure u

of. Of which they can

cure u. Which they can

control eradicate make vanish.

Th pre-lineup 4 vouchers 4

online tickets goes round 2

blocks. In about 35 years

there will be no need

4 th conventional incarceratory forms

a non-virtual society uses. Is

being sent 2 another continent

2 marry a bit similar

2 being banished? Is there

a voice in ur head

telling u there is a

voice in ur head asking

a voice in ur head

2 head 4 th hills?

If so. Without delay. There's

that crow now down on

green grass. He or it's

with another crow. Even in

th outback this's a particularly

pretty morn. Watch I am

going 2 put on my

invisibility cloak. It's a cloud-covered

shiver running thru my tendrils

n each toenail I have

lurches a little 4ward like

a fiddlehead smiling. If one

has odours these can b

compared 2. If dressed like

a rodent. Gait of amphibianic

ne'er-do-wells. Others have a destiny

that calls out 4 conga

lines. In trust I crow.

When they want u 2

leave sometimes they FedEx a

letter. Or send big bouquets

of hay n ragweed. Other

times th gang gathers (together)

like an ethics panel n

puts u into a humid

thermoradiant chair in front of

them n says defend urself.

Say something, a crow inside

ur head echoes. Say u

didn't mean it, say u

were confused temporarily off ur

rocker deeply rattled by something

u saw on th Interweb.

Explain u were under influence

of crowspawn. Shriek I wasn't

myself. Write ur name on

a paper 2 show how

u do it. They figure

4 minutes per client, 3

if each cuts back on

niceties. A carillon's belling

2 keep everybody on sched.

Helps. Helps. Helps. Helps. Hel.

In th middle of a

dry field uninsured workers haul

enough soil out 2 leave

a sizable hole n he

is asked 2 sleep there

4 3 weeks. A corner

@ Bay n University where

she goes with a raft

of cardboard. There's a soft

cage in th ravine ur

uncle told u about 2

years ago. He was going

thru a bad time. Ud

just left college with plans

2 see Antarctica. U got

that blank in his eyes

n for a moment he

was more than a narrative.

He was linked in. All

my online friends think I'd

look better with bangs. Well,

about 12 of them say

this n the rest don't

comment, so. All of love's

a freakin hotbed of magpies.

Makes u fancy that ravine.

Makes u singe in June

evenings as sun sweeps in2

some ditch in a dry

boneyard about 3 kms west

of th promenade where u

go with a latte from

th newest roaster place. Why

not drop bucks on ubercool

everything. Designers make th world

efficient n more attractive. Don't

get left out of what's

trending. Items that u don't

even like in a store

window can b ravishing @

sunset on 'Hula Boulevard.' Just

4get abt money cuz lack's

th real culprit, not excess.

U know there's Prozac in
that creekbank. Lurking leakage. Downers
in bathwater. Some of this
mirrors th psychic load of
disciplining others. Go immediately 2

ur room. I told u
2 get 2 ur room
n stay there until I
tell u 2 free urself.
March! Until March? No. March!

He says, I'm banned from
th alleyway. Cop said if
I come back there I
get arrested, that's it. No
more warnings. Set one foot

on th premises of th
duplex u once lived in
n then craved 2 much
n, well, ur going 2
be apprehended n charged, with

prejudice. We're watching u closely.

Delectate on that b4 u

go 2 dreamland 2night, guy.

Th kitchen is out of

bounds for those with a

carb issue. Bathroom's supervised by

a fulltime attendant in case

the bingers try 2. Well,

it's an All-U-Can-Eat joint, attracts

th upchuckers. @ any rate,

those bitches b hoarding. Word.

Thirsty crow's gotta go 4

th baubles in garbage. These

sculptures r fragile n so

th grey ribbon keeps u

back. What do u think

it's there 4? This is

my lane. What r u

a fuckin idiot? This is

my lane.

4. WISH

Every leaf on that tree

looks like a small hand

typing. Suddenly th tree

seems entirely inflamed! All of

nature a diarist.

2 banish.

2 vanish.

4 one or

th other,

2 wish.

REPLENISH

a solo

Fan n a bottle of water kept replenished from th tap

Quiet room that u keep replenishing with ur greed 4 it

Books replenished by repeat reading n rereadings that change their
meaning limits

Love 4 th ones u love now who can it seems only ever evade ur
replenishing want

Is it that u had it n lost it or cannot believe in ever having unless it is
right here in ur palms btween ur breasts n thighs

Is it that u don't know how 2 love n break it all 2 crumbs over n over again

Shades pulled so light jiggles under th last possible half-foot of
windowspace

Piles of books in cubby shelves n air flaps taunting reread my meaning limit

Bright tongue of sun on every treeleaf waggling about solitude being 4

th weakminded

U want 2 replenish ur heat hearing heart

Want 2 love th one n th other with similar constancy (but suck @ this)

Pink hydrangeas simply flopped over with all th waters they can't help

but gorge on again n again as if blind 2 all th droughtstricken weeds

@ their ankles

Ur mother, with language

Ur father with blood, also

A hard beige desktop 2 which u have added a few sepia mug prints

Th flickering of cuntlust in u when reading writing watching all th small

shining tongues in th courtyard

This is a day that gets replaced by all th ones 2 come

Clean slates, clean dates

Nobody gets brought back like Alkestis it's just a dream or thoughtcontour

2 help th living go on with their steps 2ward a black banishment (this

written th last day u were 49, rather grim)

2 months of th tragedians played off against numerous bus trips 2 aphasia

Ull replenish ur autobiography as u c fit then sleep late 2 dream a last little

wild one

2 redream a little wild tongue

As if being chronicled matters 2 th tree @ all, or does it?

N then came th last thgin n

yad in that place n she had

2 evael now. I picked up various

papers n binders n books n sehtolc

n cups n glasses. There were places

in th swodniw she could still look

out from 2 c th courtdray. I

listened 2 th sevaw of splashing water.

Fountains r now essential if a lake

is dekcal. She considered coming here skeew

ago n how could it have neeb

so many weeks. Is time real. Is

th body only ysub when awake? Really

tried 2 abate my evol 4 th

lost one but o llew it persists

calls out sirenlike. I derats in2 windows

of others. I stare ereht. She is

so beautiful some syad on many she

disgusts me. That is th case 4

th htrae itself with its gnitautculf

attractions. Am I ladit. Am I not

tidal. Llits she dillydallies picking up paper
pads, snioc, pencils. Discourages herself
from ever gnivael wonders where 2 go
txen. How is it light
will llaf on her, n th coming
speels will soothe. I love 2 ynam
2 b enola yet how I want
loneness 4 a tcirts diet now. Women
r always thought of as th srevig,
th dehcatta ones, not th hermits. I
can raeh my deskvoice shuffling @ ksud,
scratching a tnelis wall with delighted perversities.
Renol. Resol. Revol. Aloft n alive perhaps
4 a week more of introspection. Th
earth sdeen inspecting. As does her traeh.
I talk of gnihtyreve n rather little.
Further into this episode she skaerb a
glass on th towel rack n begins
niaga 2 read Christensen's *Alphabet* aloud. I

                                    exist.

Play

Excess is the culprit.
Euripedes, trans. Anne Carson

hard to say whether it's really really late or really really early.
Earlate.
January 4, 2012 at 7:22

It was really friggin early. And now the day is very wonked.
January 4, 2012 at 15:01

library vibrancy; solo silence silo, my kind of shush.
January 11, 2012 at 16:31

Reading family geneology in four directions that each loop
around to crisscross the others, sort of like the dog's
meander-tracks out on the lakesnow yesterday
January 17, 2012 at 17:21

simmer down kiddo.
January 20, 2012 at 13:10

only bright spot of the last 3 days was provided by the
sizzling hot female paramedics.
January 23, 2012 at 00:58

has to comment on the huge infrastructure of sense-making
involved in a sentence like the above. We take it for granted,
every second.
January 24, 2012 at 19:42

tearing through journals from 1984–1991; recognize one's past
self is probably the best mentor at many points.
January 27, 2012 at 12:00

really frickin irritating dreams.
February 4, 2012 at 11:53

slow reading has another name. it's reading.
February 7, 2012 at 12:04

too much enough not enough much too little. and over. revise
the measure.
March 1, 2012 at 11:38

is running a mok a pparently today.
March 4, 2012 at 16:52

see there's nowhere inperson speech you can walk up to
somebody and say excess = x s. s'why I love the internet.
March 8, 2012 at 14:21

considering the chasm so often between carers and careers.

March 12, 2012 at 17:31

after being away several days, opens up the kitchen computer
and finds a 'How to make a fried egg' video link. The kids are
all right indeed.

March 19, 2012 at 14:44

biking silken wind or what.

March 20, 2012 at 13:29

saw forsythia on the way to see cynthia.

March 24, 2012 at 15:56

jop-drawed by those hills. who made such hills? how do those
hills hold? dam-wild hill action.

April 5, 2012 at 16:49

each ache each aches.

April 19, 2012 at 12:52

wrioting.

April 19, 2012 at 15:10

trying to think outside the bosc.

April 25, 2012 at 4:21

famous first words.

April 25, 2012 at 16:33

oasisish.

April 28, 2012 at 11:25

accordion: full pedal jacket.

May 2, 2012 at 9:21

swall swallow wallow allow low ow: the draw of words has its
own progressions ... always furious and lurid and turgid and so
it goes onword.

May 3, 2012 at 9:29

Hitchcock's Marnie is the bomb.

May 4, 2012 at 16:11

good morning sweetie, might you have something on that
smells like chocolate and coconut, there's a certain waft ....
Well, mom, it's called Be Enchanted, so.

May 6, 2012 at 1:13

dreamt the twins were 2, one under each of my arms, wriggling
on a couch the way we used to. Silas says, dreams are real
when you're having them, mom.

May 7, 2012 at 9:53

hmm, what DOES one wear to a first class in Trojan tragedy?

May 8, 2012 at 1:31

Just watched beautiful mother-daughter bed clip from Akerman's
Les Rendez-vous d'Anna on YouTube and at the same time
daughter sends me Jon Hamm answers girls questions video and
I so watched it too. Both excellent.

May 12, 2012 at 00:40

sounds of moving water watery moving of sounds moving
sounds of water. water moving.

May 17, 2012 at 9:27

strength it takes to stick to your words.

May 19, 2012 at 9:23

Attention Trucks Turning. Watch out for those Attention Trucks!

May 21, 2012 at 15:02

lioves.

May 28, 2012 at 19:46

around here they turn 15. cakes exist.

June 3, 2012, at 8:42

rereading Anne Carson's bitchin 'The Gender of Sound'
essay. 'The main responsibility for funeral lament had
belonged to women from earliest Greek times ... Yet lawgivers
of the 6th and 5th centuries ... were at pains to restrict these
female outpourings to a minimum of sound and emotional
display ... Laws were passed specifying the location, time,
duration, personnel, choreography, musical content and verbal
content of the women's funeral lament on the grounds that
these "harsh and barbaric sounds" were a stimulus to
"disorder and license."' Sound topical?

June 5, 2012 at 17:36

& just for the record, someone handed me a baby in a dream
last night. I said, um, me?

June 5, 2012 at 18:03

po v etry.

June 7, 2012 at 9:53

walk in my house and the rap playing says; fellatio
interference promiscuous homo sapiens

June 7, 2012 at 11:04

1 2 3 4 1/2 hours of Glass/Wilson/Childs leads to 1 2 3 4 5 6 7
hours of insane dreamstew. If it could be fresh.

June 10, 2012 at 1:22

imagining young Avril Lavigne as Iphigenia. And Cobain, at the
end, as Orestes. Both singing Mama take this badge offa me.

June 11, 2012 at 18:18

the beauty and challenge of facebook is that it is an absolutely
smeared space of the veiled/regaled and the displayed/played.

June 18, 2012 at 1:58

heat, sweat, etc.

June 20, 2012 at 13:12

interiorate; deteriority.

June 21, 2012 at 9:54

that special drowsy snarly fuck off from the back of the bus ...
ah, nostalgic.

July 3, 2012 at 11:11

is noticing more often that anytime there's any kind of
conversation about anything in this country it's called a brouhaha.

July 9, 2012 at 2:59

you got your desire in/on one hand, and your loss in/on the
other, and the two hands keep smashing up against each other
like a music box monkey's cymbals. That, my margaret, is
consciousness. Hear it crash!

July 24, 2012 at 11:52

now to make an excellent salad.

July 25, 2012 at 18:13

4 pm train horn a blowin. then chuggachuggachugga.

July 30, 2012 at 15:55

suppressing the yen to kiss my sleeping daughter's feet.

July 31, 2012 at 11:13

ohohoh what a lotta moonlight can do.
August 1, 2012 at 19:03

gnossos songs.
August 4, 2012 at 00:26

dniw niwd iwdn wdni all askew.
August 5, 2012 at 13:12

the benefit of teens staying up till 2:30 am on summer nights
is that they sleep their faces off all morning. I tiptoe around
on little mom feet, drink coffee, think, write and read. (oh,
that's my work, for all those who think I do nothing.)
August 8, 2012 at 9:53

coming into toronto last night, side-by-side signs:
BAGEL | BIO GEL
August 9, 2012 at 17:55

drainched.
August 14, 2012 at 13:30

chaoasis.
August 16, 2012 at 17:54

buyological impairative
August 17, 2012 at 8:28

hearing phrases from glass's einstein on the beach in the
mount rushmore climax of north by northwest.
August 19, 2012 at 22:32

get home with cold beer look in mirror peer prominent black
smears under both eyes from Layton tribute.
August 22, 2012 at 20:09

at times like these all you can do is hope the kids have
brains about storms. hoping.
August 27, 2012 at 2:38

beaiouty
August 29, 2012 at 1:26

little that depresses me more than being asked to vote
for the best poem
September 2, 2012 at 1:54

just sitting here on facebook ... and i know that my kittens will
lead me on ...
September 2, 2012 at 13:07

curious relative passages.
September 3, 2012 at 14:32
cu ri ou sr el at iv ep as sa ge s.
September 3, 2012 at 14:33
at cu el ep ge iv ou ri s sa sr.
September 3, 2012 at 14:35
rsassir uoviegpe leuctasa.
September 3, 2012 at 14:38
recessive ovum pollutants.
September 3, 2012 at 14:40
took 7 minutes of my own life.
September 3, 2012 at 14:40

now now now now now now now now now now
September 11, 2012 at 8:53
persuasion sway suede. some people say wordplay is not
interesting but i think it is everything for it is writing in the ear
which is listening to itself become itself, and therefore selfcritical,
selfaudible and aware of the others the proximate the adjacent
and imminent. and as you offered with hear her here it quickly
also becomes very libidinal, multiply directional, defeating binary
structures between interlocutors such as us here hers hearing.
September 12, 2012 at 11:09

facebook status
aabcefko ossttu
sutatsko obecaf
September 15, 2012 at 22:51
thinking about how writers have always been derided for
wasting time in cafés. on terraces. patioslackers. And now we're
told it's a waste of time to be on facebook. But there's enough
that's new and intriguing about the poetics of this polyvocal
improvisational milieu that I feel I learn from it. Present.
Presenth. If only someone would bring me my absinthe.
September 16, 2012 at 15:25

why does flarf parse only the most base and banal of the
internet when we can parse anything anything as if there's
something less valid about the brilliant
September 17, 2012 at 11:00

all hail broke loose.
September 17, 2012 at 20:30

odd ode
ddd eoo
edo ddo
September 19, 2012 at 9:11

'Demand for The Clock is expected to be high so please
expect significant wait times.'
September 21, 2012 at 1:29

brain feeling a little on the verge of.
September 26, 2012 at 11:15

aabee eeeeffg g hiiill ln nno orrtt tv.
September 26, 2012 at 13:57

foegr evehtno e lttila gn ile efnia rb.
September 26, 2012 at 13:59

selftrust eflrssttu tsurtfles
September 26, 2012 at 22:21

Please maintain control of your personal property at all times.
What???
September 27, 2012 at 2:48

enotsat tesor
aeenoor ssttt
rosetta stone
September 28, 2012 at 19:17

the phonetic charge of every phrase
aac ceeeeeef ghhhhi no opprr rsttvy
esa rhpyreve foegra hc citen ohpeht
September 29, 2012 at 6:09

rain in Bath which seems about right.
October 2, 2012 at 12:27

clitoris, solicitor.
cciiiill, ooorrsstt.
roticilo, ssirotilc.
October 3, 2012 at 18:11
on a six week trip visiting sites significant to my grandmothers'
early lives before they emigrated, one from britain, one from
greece, both 1914–15 at the age of 15. And thinking about
autobiography, self-narrativity and girls' changing self-
display practices over several eras.
October 6, 2012 at 19:06

membrane in the brine. (for karim)
October 9, 2012 at 14:28
arising to the window of her subjectivity
abcdeee fg hhi iiiijn no oor rssttttuvwwy
ytivitc ej bus rehfow od niw ehtotgnisira
October 13, 2012 at 9:10

thrilled to be at the Odeon of Herodes Atticus; note the 'ode'
in odeon
October 14, 2012 at 9:32
awake; it's still dark
aaade; iik kllrs st'tw
kradl; lit sst'ie kawa
October 14, 2012 at 23:46

siren einrs neris
October 16, 2012 at 5:14
not jazz; how abt sum female vocal trance
aaa aabc cee efh jll mmnnoo orstt tuvwzz;
ecn artl avo vel ame fmustb awohz; zajton
October 16, 2012 at 5:52

the antiquities are breathrobbing but the wifi is, alas, forshit.
October 18, 2012 at 14:47
elektra i am on your side girl
aadeeeg i ii kl lmno orrr stuy
lrigedi s ru oy noma iart kele
October 18, 2012 at 16:17

eating peanuts at a hotel in delphi.
October 19, 2012 at 12:51
please bat some puns around with me to balance out my
brain; the beauty's killing me. antiquity's quitting me.
October 19, 2012 at 12:56

a colossal limestone female head
October 20, 2012 at 11:53
is brainzonked, or to put it in greek,
metadekapitroniekronopolitisi. hha.
October 22, 2012 at 4:57

single czech ladies
accdee eghii llnssz
seidal hcezc elgnis
October 23, 2012 at 3:47
swam in the aegean
October 24, 2012 at 1:22
lightning, thunder, streaming rain the whole night; cycladic
baptismal
October 24, 2012 at 2:38
do I look LACONIC enough?
October 28, 2012 at 11:10
tonight in athens saw an unending stream of citizens
coherently hitting the streets, young people, elderly people,
many workers, families.
November 7, 2012 at 19:20
rome = over-the-knee leather boots.
November 8, 2012 at 12:19

dormituttimatini.
November 11, 2012 at 5:12
just realized why the cat obsession on facebook: CHAT.
November 12, 2012 at 3:40

chaos and order
aacdd ehn oorrs
redro dna soahc
November 18, 2012 at 1:48

um, can I go back.
November 19, 2012 at 11:44

mirror l rorrim
imorrr l rrromi
rorrim l mirror
November 24, 2012 at 22:31

thanks Anne for connecting me to Tiny Furniture. Crisscrossing
Fat Girl, High Art and My So-Called Life, etc.
Can't believe I hadn't seen this.
December 1, 2012 at 2:38

Maybe it's a poor replica.
Aaabc eei i lmoo pprrst'y.
Acilp err o opas t'iebyam.
December 3, 2012 at 14:49

a bunch of feminists
a bceff hi imnnosstu
s tsini me ffohcnuba
December 6, 2012 at 14:33

proud to have raised feminist sons.
December 6, 2012 at 15:05

that satisfying feeling of suddenly seeing a dozen easy edits.
letting it change. letting it become something else entire.
December 12, 2012 at 11:02

now actively repeat it all
December 15, 2012 at 18:09

did u think i had forgotten u
add d efghh i iik nnoortttu u
une t togro f dah iknihtudi d
December 18, 2012 at 1:48

just came up with an awesome constraint.
December 18, 2012 at 16:56

If there's one thing that lightens my mood it's overhearing
genius shower singing
December 19, 2012 at 22:04

everoreveroreveroreverie
December 25, 2012 at 23:40

just simulread Idle No More as I Die No More.
December 29, 2012 at 14:28

2012, we had a time.
December 31, 2012 at 12:28
the horizon of the desirable; walk in that direction
aaa bcddeee ee fhh hhiiiiikl; lnnn oo oorr rstttttwz
noi tceridt ah tni klawelbar; ised eh tfon oziroheht
January 1, 2013 at 22:23
Moribund Facekvetch Hey Margaret,
January 1, 2013 at 22:58
Moribund Facekvetch are these part of a larger project.
Reragel jepcoetr?
January 1, 2013 at 22:59
Margaret Christakos each is a meditative construction that i
build in realtime as i am posting; i compose them according to
the constraint of a lyric phrase that resonates within a variety
of thematic areas, which is then reordered as an alphabetic
translation, and then as palindrome of the original phrase using
its letter count template. point is it's not random, rather highly
dictated and yet the result is a wild unassimilable kind of
foreign currency ... as a cumulative composition the individual
pieces gain narrative dimensions, invite oral performance, and
draw me into a deeper contemplation of simultilingualism ...
so yes esy sey
January 1, 2013 at 23:10
John Barlow my mind zipped out vividly internally auditorially
with that one and it sounded like busy queen st w in just such
weather as today
January 1, 2013 at 23:13
Margaret Christakos i like these things where you have to
count and think a lot about what must come next given what
has been agreed upon in relation to the act to be enacted ...
January 1, 2013 at 23:15
Moribund Facekvetch Interesting how the pile-on of multiple
letters moves quicker, changes one's reading. Burns into song

or chant. or something else.

January 1, 2013 at 23:16

Margaret Christakos and they are so difficult to vocalize, i have to remember how to read and phoneticize, like coming to the language anew each time, i like that very much

January 1, 2013 at 23:17

Margaret Christakos and gary, one other thing, my mother suffered very bad paraphasia after a stroke last year so that her speech became inextricably tousled and extrapresent and erased at the same moment. in many cases there were transposed and substituted phonemes, but also an utterly unconstrained plethora of baffled pattern – it seemed to be entirely aleatory. and yet the brain is doing something, imposing some system of recasting what is being intended and what is produced ... i began to think about how wouldn't it be interesting if all of the letters in an intended phrase were actually faithful to the original but reordered to the point where no human could, in a moment of listening attentively, with any degree of practice at mastering this, decipher the original or intended utterance. i guess it has led me to think about how unprepared we are, at most junctures, to recognize even the known when it is presented in unfamiliar forms ...

January 1, 2013 at 23:35

Moribund Facekvetch I think about how a musical instrument or a body is an interface to thought, language and experience.

January 1, 2013 at 23:37

Margaret Christakos and a translation environment gets us into that space where there's more than one reading/hearing going on at any moment, which immediately allows us to value multiplicity over the right or only meaning ...

January 1, 2013 at 23:40

Moribund Facekvetch I wonder about a changing/evolving system of 'translation' where it's not only alphabetic ordering or palindromic, but other organizing systems that bend and yield and resist in different ways.

January 1, 2013 at 23:51

Margaret Christakos for sure, reordering possibilities abound!

January 1, 2013 at 23:57

a camera not yet taking pictures but a voice recorder on a
silent beach though a battery rolling under a chesterfield since
January 3, 2013 at 11:18

held the broom crosswise to excavate a mordant debt to patron
council administrators who stewed chinese apple cores into a
daft laundry chute and

January 4, 2013 at 10:05

a very mid-1980s Jack Layton sat in my tent with me
last night; just reporting the dreamfacts
January 4, 2013 at 22:20

put up a parking lot
aag ik l noppprt tuu
tol gn i krapapu tup
January 4, 2013 at 22:23

kind of a bitch
abcd fh i iknot
hcti ba f odnik
January 8, 2013 at 12:25

sophtnesc
January 9, 2013 at 12:22

ntnsfcayshun
January 10, 2013 at 10:11

wrap up ur troubles in ur old text-bag n
aabb de eg illnnoop pr rr rst tt-uuuuw x
ngab t-x et dlorunis el bu ort rupupar w
January 14, 2013 at 11:15

jay-z luvs u more than u will kno
January 14, 2013 at 13:57

4 the hound: killing ma softly
4 ade fghhi: iklllmn no osttuy
y utt soonn: mlllkii hh gfade4
y lft osamg: nillikd nu oheht4
January 15, 2013 at 11:05

116

i saw the best minds of my generation giving it away for free.
January 16, 2013 at 14:17

imagine caring abt an e-message more than buying an suv
January 17, 2013 at 00:42

jus sittin on th book uv th face, wastin time
aab ceefhh ii ii jkmn nn oo osss, tttttt uuvw
emi tnitsa we ca fhtv uk oo bhtn, onitti ssuj
January 18, 2013 at 1:47

one year aee nory rae yeno
January 20, 2013 at 12:10

hopes i made them fall fill fell foll full in love with Alphabet
January 23, 2013 at 9:07

ur soakin in it now!
ai iiknnn oo rs tuw!
wo ntinin ik ao sur!
January 23, 2013 at 11:46

inventriloqui. eventriloquoi.
January 24, 2013 at 21:42

wordinary
January 25, 2013 at 15:48

o see can you say: say yes say yes sey yas sey yas. know no
know no know now kno now. no yes say now. sey now yas kno.
repeat.
January 27, 2013 at 13:10

syllabia
January 27, 2013 at 13:38

vocaholic
January 27, 2013 at 13:40

fact fect fict foct fuct
January 27, 2013 at 13:42

emopome is probably better, referencing ideopome, as well as
being palindnilap.
January 28, 2013 at 1:59

itkicking
January 29, 2013 at 11:00

utopia utopie utopii utopio utopiu
uipotu oipotu iipotu eipotu aipotu
– a brief solo from 'utopiano'
January 30, 2013 at 16:13

multitumultitumultitumultitudes
January 31, 2013 at 14:47
so radically dishevelled – adjusting to caprice
aa aacccdddd eeeeghiiiij – llllnoopr rs ssttuvy
ec irpacotgn itsujdadell – evehsidyl la cidaros [berlant]
February 1, 2013 at 2:01

bodydob ydobody
bbbdddd ooooyyy
ydobody bodydob
February 1, 2013 at 2:05
doing, going. going, doing.
going doing going.
going doing doing going. how
it's going. it's dewing.
February 3, 2013 at 1:38

godogodogodogodogodogodogodogo. do.
February 3, 2013 at 1:41
gooddogooddogooddogooddogooder.
February 3, 2013 at 1:42

so not twitter. you read it and you read it again. you read it
again and you are reading it. gains.
February 7, 2013 at 1:43
tasty stati!!
February 7, 2013 at 11:36

and you are reading it.
aaa dde eeg iinnorr ty.
tig nid aer erauoyd na.
February 7, 2013 at 3:27
i took one sentence and threaded it through another and
all i got was this lousy t-shirt
February 7, 2013 at 22:11

mul ult lti tid idu dud ude des
February 8, 2013 at 10:06

you dirgebag.
February 8, 2013 at 10:09

reciprocal n expectant
aaccceeeil n nopprrttx
tnatcepxen l acorpicer
February 13, 2013 at 18:43

lo er
February 14, 2013 at 14:54

the ways a book contains all the thoughts that made it have
covers on its recognitions allows my mind 2 incandesce its
seams n ripple, dawg
February 16, 2013 at 12:05

[spoiler alert] too soon it ends
February 17, 2013 at 11:55

hahha even if this distinction remains fragile and enigmatic,
allow me to treat it as established, in order to save time
February 17, 2013 at 16:14

o yes i play the homophone, n u?
February 18, 2013 at 10:05

holler of mirrors ...
February 19, 2013 at 14:19

H
February 23, 2013 at 15:45

writing makes u burn ur frozen pizza.
February 25, 2013 at 16:22

does anyone else think 7 hours of continuous writing time is
a fucking miracle likely never to bear its own repetition ...
February 27, 2013 at 11:42

in a way facebook is striking
me more n more as flipper
side of found poetics; everyone upstalling
their texts 4 grabz. a huge
conceptual shift 4 individuals 2 loose
speech material 4 gleaning. once u

have more than 200 'friends' u
have fully accepted the premise that
u do not in any sense
know whuz reading u or whatz
being made of ur output. is
different from publishing; tis a set
of display play replay relations waggled
in small parcels of language, entirely
excessive n recessive n sort of
flagrante. but my coffee's ready, so.
February 27, 2013 at 21:31

thinks teenaged girls must have been the inspiration for the
internet: they are the zenith of everybody talking and listening
simultaneously.
March 2, 2013 at 13:41

do u ment
March 10, 2013 at 11:15

girls gilrs slrig
gggii illlr rrsss
girls srlig slrig
March 18, 2013 at 10:09

communal, communicable
March 25, 2013 at 9:55

facebook is a little timelapse fast lap from the poetics of direct
confessional lyric address to metalyric practices of indirect
documentary, constraint and conceptualism, due in large part
to a negotiation with the audience/public/commons as
both known and anonymous
March 28, 2013 at 9:36

let's pretend we're anonymous
adee ee'elmnn noop rrsst'tuwy
suom ynonaer e'wdn eterpst'el
March 28, 2013 at 9:40

anonymous unanimous
enunamuys ynenomuys
inynemyas aninumyas
onanimaes enonymaes
unenomeis inunameis
yninumios onynemios
anonymous unanimous
March 28, 2013 at 9:50
         pirsunel porsynil pursanol pyrsenul parsinyl personal
March 28, 2013 at 9:56
economy uv da personal _c_n_m_ _v d_ p_rs_n_l
March 28, 2013 at 9:58
         let's portend you're unanimous.
k that's it for now. seeya.
March 28, 2013 at 10:00

Intheafternoon

Intheafternoon of a day

Intheafternoon of a day of institched thinking

Intheafternoon of a day of institched thinking 4 the corollary

Intheafternoon of a day of institched thinking 4 the corollary of voice

Intheafternoon of a day's breath of institched thinking 4 the corollary
of voice in photographs

Intheafternoon of an aftermath

Intheafternoon of a choir swaying toward a gratuitous affection

In the corollary of all thaeiour quiet

In the space of thaeiour institched voices all the unsame

thought's luminous

NOTES AND ACKNOWLEDGEMENTS

Thank you to Susan Holbrook, Leigh Nash, Alana Wilcox, Jeramy Dodds, Evan Munday and everyone at Coach House Books. Thanks to Bryan Gee for collaborating on the cover design. Love to Bryan, Zephyr, Silas and Clea. Thanks to Gary Barwin/Moribund Facekvetch and John Barlow for making cameo appearances.

This work was composed between 2008 and 2013. An earlier draft of 'Threshold' was included in *New American Poetry*. 'Banished' appeared in *Event*. Younger versions of 'Enough' and 'We' are online at ditch.ca. Some of the texts in the 'Weapon' series appeared in TOK. Thank you to the editors. 'Play' is composed of real time.

Thanks for essential funding to the George Woodcock Fund for Writers (Writers' Trust); to the Ontario Arts Council; to the Canada Council for the Arts; and to the Chalmers Foundation for a generous fellowship in 2012–2013. Appreciation to Massey College, Toronto, for a writing retreat space in Spring 2012. Thanks to guides and hosts during research travels in England and Greece in Fall 2012. Ongoing thanks to family for additional financial assistance.

Sincere thanks and affection to the many: numerous individuals for stimulation and community over the writing period; friends and mentors; to Mary Jane Christakos and my brothers and sister; students I have worked with over these years; dear companions virtual and vital; longstanding participants in Influency Salon whose generous engagements with both the course and the online magazine made manifest and shareable its success; and many among my near and nearer multitudes for ideas, alphabets, meanderings and provocations.

GRATITUDE

ADEGIRTTU

EDUTITARG